90S POP QUIZ

Tim Tyrrell

Cover designed by Cover Designer

Tim Tyrrell
Visit my website at www.timtyrrell.com

Printed in the United States of America

First Printing: Aug 2023
Tim Tyrrell

ISBN-9798856396507

For Gary

Other books by Tim Tyrrell:

The Name Dropper

The Oliver Factor

80s Pop Quiz

Friends Pop Quiz

1

What fictional town is the setting for the movie "Scream"?

2

In 1997, what longtime game show introduced a new digital puzzle board?

3

Who released the song "My Love Is Your Love" in 1998?

4

Who died after a car crash in a Paris tunnel in 1997?

5

In what German city was Monica Seles stabbed on court in 1993 by Gunter Parche?

6

What was Jodie Foster's character's name in the movie "The Silence of the Lambs"?

7

What opened in 1994 that linked the United Kingdom and France?

8

What song sings about a "black fly in your Chardonnay"?

9

Who wrote the book "Angela's Ashes: A Memoir" that became a best seller when it was released in 1996?

10

Who wrote the song "Nothing Compares 2 U" that became a number one song in over 20 countries for Sinead O'Connor in 1990?

11

Who was the President of Russia from 1991 to 1999?

12

What animated TV show created by Mike Judge debuted on MTV in 1993?

13

What was the first Number One song of the 1990s on the Billboard Hot 100 Chart?

14

What theme park opened in France in 1992?

8

"Ironic" by Alanis Morissette

9

Frank McCourt

10

Prince

11

Boris Yeltsin

12

"Beavis and Butthead"

13

"Another Day in Paradise" by Phil Collins

14

Euro Disney Resort (now known as Disneyland Paris)

15

What was the name of Mariah Carey's 1994 Album that featured the song "All I Want for Christmas Is You"?

16

What was the name of the shopping center that opened in Minnesota in 1992 that became the largest in the United States?

17

Who was Bill Clinton's Vice-President?

18

Where were the 1996 Summer Olympics held?

19

What Musical group sang the song "No Scrubs"?

20

What was the name of the Space Shuttle that docked with the Russian Mir Space Station in 1995?

21

Who played the title character in the TV Series "Felicity"?

22

Who directed the 1993 movie "A Bronx Tale"?

23

Why wasn't the World Series played in 1994?

24

Who were the members of the Musical group The Fugees?

25

Who starred as Vivian Ward in the movie "Pretty Woman"?

26

Who was the lead prosecutor for the State of California in the O.J. Simpson trial?

27

Who did Michael Jackson marry in 1994 and then divorce the next year?

21
Keri Russell

22
Robert DeNiro

23
Major League Baseball was on strike

24
Lauren Hill, Wyclef Jean and Pras Michel

25
Julia Roberts

26
Marcia Clark

27
Lisa Marie Presley

28

Who was released from prison after 27 years and then elected President of South Africa in 1994?

29

What was Ross and Monica's last name on the TV Series "Friends"?

30

Who played James Bond throughout the 1990s?

31

Who won the 1999 World Series?

32

What was created when the Maastricht Treaty went into effect on November 1, 1993?

33

What Rock band was featured in the Disney theme park ride Rock 'n' Roller Coaster that opened in 1999?

28
Nelson Mandela

29
Gellar

30
Pierce Brosnan

31
The New York Yankees

32
The European Union

33
Aerosmith

34

What two brothers were part of the Pop Group 98 Degrees?

35

What was the name of the comet that was visible to the naked eye that made its
closest approach to Earth in 1997?

36

What kind of business did Hugh Grant's character William Thacker own in the
movie "Notting Hill"?

37

Who won the 1994 FIFA World Cup that took place in the United States?

38

Who played Chili Palmer in the film "Get Shorty"?

39

Who released the single "O.P.P." in 1991?

40

In what city did the first season of MTV's "The Real World" take place?

41

What 90s Girl Group released the album "Funky Divas"?

42

In what city was the Good Friday Agreement signed, that ended the violence in Northern Ireland?

43

Who was featured on the cover of Time Magazine next to the words "Yep, I'm Gay"?

44

What was the name of the 1996 sequel to "Escape From New York" that brought Kurt Russell back as Snake Plissken?

45

What actress and comedian starred in the music video for "Low" from the band Cracker?

46

What was the name of the toy where the user had to feed a small virtual pet, or it would die?

47

What technology was made available to the public in August of 1991?

48

Who was the lead singer of the group The Wallflowers, who had a very famous father named Bob?

49

What was the name of the White House intern that Bill Clinton had an affair with?

50

What was the name of the 1992 book by Madonna that featured erotic photographs?

51

Which figure skater was attacked and had her knee bashed with a baton?

52

Which heartthrob who played Dr. Doug Ross left the medical drama "ER" in 1999?

53

Who sang the national anthem at Super Bowl XXV in 1991?

54

Which female talk show, created by Barbara Walters, debuted in 1997?

55

What Heavy Metal band released the record "Reload" in 1997?

56

Who joined the TV Series "Melrose Place" in 1993 as Amanda Woodward?

57

Who played Ben Sanderson in the 1995 movie "Leaving Las Vegas"?

58

In June of 1995, Hugh Grant was arrested in Los Angeles for soliciting the services of Estella Marie Thompson. What name was she better known by?

59

What professional tennis player born in Yugoslavia became a U.S. citizen in 1994?

60

Who was the NBA Most Valuable Player in 1991, 1992, 1996 and 1998?

61

What Tony Danza comedy ended its eight-year run in 1992?

62

Who played Eva Peron in the 1996 film "Evita"?

63

In a 1999 episode of "Friends", what one word did Ross keep yelling when trying to move a couch up a staircase?

64

What nighttime Soap Opera aired its final episodes in 1993 after 14 seasons?

65

What was the name of the woman who accused U.S. Supreme Court nominee Clarence Thomas of sexual harassment in 1991?

66

In what area of Florida does the movie "The Birdcage" take place?

67

Who became Prime Minister of the United Kingdom after Margaret Thatcher resigned in 1990?

68

Who played Joel Fleischman in the TV Series "Northern Exposure"?

69

What cable channel was created by Rupert Murdoch and launched in 1996?

70

What 90s band hit number one in the UK and number five in the USA singing about the film "Breakfast at Tiffany's"?

71

Who directed the 1994 film "Quiz Show"?

72

Who played the Walsh twins on "Beverly Hills, 90210"?

73

What song did Elton John rework and sing at the funeral for Princess Diana?

74

Who wrote the number one children's book "Millie's Book" that was released in 1990?

75

Which music icon took his own life in April of 1994 at age 27?

69

Fox News Channel

70

Deep Blue Something

71

Robert Redford

72

Jason Priestly and Shannen Doherty

73

"Candle in the Wind"

74

Barbara Bush

75

Kurt Cobain

76

What kind of vehicle was O.J. Simpson in, during the low-speed chase from the police that was televised live?

77

What singer passed away in November 1991 from complications from AIDS?

78

In the movie "Romy and Michele's High School Reunion", what did the duo claim to invent?

79

Which member of the Kennedy family was tried and acquitted of a 1991 rape charge?

80

Who played Dr. Melfi on the HBO Series "The Sopranos"?

81

What television network launched on January 6, 1995, with the pilot episode of "Star Trek: Voyager"?

82

Who joined the TV drama "NYPD Blue" in 1994 as Detective Bobby Simone?

76
White Ford Bronco

77
Freddie Mercury

78
Post-It Notes

79
William Kennedy Smith

80
Lorraine Bracco

81
United Paramount Network (UPN)

82
Jimmy Smits

83

Which two singers had a number one hit in America and a number two hit in the UK with the 1998 song "The Boy Is Mine"?

84

What was the name of the movie released in 1997 that starred The Spice Girls?

85

Which President was inaugurated on January 20, 1993?

86

What show debuted on HBO and starred James Gandolfini and Edie Falco?

87

In 1992, who appeared on the game show "Sale of the Century", two years before he was murdered along with Nicole Brown Simpson?

88

Which member of The Beatles was knighted by Queen Elizabeth in 1997?

89

In 1999, what TV recording device was introduced?

83
Brandy and Monica

84
"Spice World"

85
Bill Clinton

86
"The Sopranos"

87
Ronald Goldman

88
Paul McCartney

89
TiVo

90
What film asked the question, "do you understand the words that are coming out of my mouth"?

91
What animal did Adam Sandler wrestle for his golf ball in the film "Happy Gilmore"?

92
What was the name of the man who was beaten by police in California and videotaped that lead to the Los Angeles riots after the officers were acquitted?

93
Who played Doris Murphy in the film "A League of Their Own"?

94
Who climbed on top of David Letterman's desk and flashed her breasts at him in 1995?

95
What was the name of the place in Illinois where Wayne and Garth lived in the movie "Wayne's World"?

96
What country did Iraq invade in 1990 that lead to the Gulf War?

90
"Rush Hour"

91
An alligator

92
Rodney King

93
Rosie O'Donnell

94
Drew Barrymore

95
Aurora

96
Kuwait

97

In the film "Four Weddings and a Funeral", which of the main friends dies?

98

What did the letters A O L stand for?

99

In which state do the characters on "That 70s Show" live?

100

What was the first show to debut on the WB Television Network in 1995?

101

Who played "Buffy, the Vampire Slayer" in the original 1992 film?

102

What was the name of the auction website that launched in 1995?

103

Who sang the theme song from the James Bond movie "Goldeneye" that was written by Bono and The Edge?

104
What were the first names of the characters that Jim Carrey and Jeff Daniels
played in "Dumb and Dumber"?

105
What was the name of the song by British band Take That, that went to number
one in over 30 countries and hit number seven on the Billboard Hot 100 chart,
making it their only hit in America?

106
What "Three's Company" star had a big screen hit with the movie "Problem
Child" in 1990?

107
In a 1992 speech, who insulted the fictional character of Murphy Brown for
having a baby without a father?

108
Who won Super Bowl XXV in 1991?

109
What TV show did Ryan Reynolds star in that aired on ABC Television starting in
1998?

110
What was the only film that Jane Fonda starred in during the 1990s?

111

What actor played twins Bill and Hugh in the movie "Mrs. Winterbourne"?

112

Who played Jerry's girlfriend Sidra on "Seinfeld"?

113

What singer released the album and song "Ray of Light"?

114

The TV show "Ellen" starring Ellen DeGeneres had a different title in the first season. What was the original name of the show?

115

What was the name of the "Peanuts" special that debuted in 1990 and has Charlie and Linus coping with a friend diagnosed with Leukemia?

116

What handheld device went on sale in 1997?

117

Who officially became the co-host of "The Today Show" alongside Bryant Gumbel in 1991?

118

Who played Forest Gump's mother?

119

Who won his last Grand Slam singles title at the 1990 Australian Open?

120

Which animated TV Series started in 1997 and follows Hank Hill and his family?

121

What band released the song "Right Here Right Now" in 1990?

122

In 1993, who did Michael Jackson grant his first TV interview in 15 years to?

123

What best-selling book was made into a 1995 movie starring Meryl Streep and
Clint Eastwood?

124

Who hit Number One on the Billboard Hot 100 Chart in 1991 with "Baby Baby"?

118

Sally Field

119

Ivan Lendl

120

"King Of the Hill"

121

Jesus Jones

122

Oprah Winfrey

123

"The Bridges of Madison County"

124

Amy Grant

125
What Broadway Musical closed at the Shubert Theater in New York City after
6,137 performances in 1990?

126
What was the name of the short-lived Soap Opera that ran from 1995 to 1997,
that was a spin-off of the show "Loving"?

127
Which Olympic Gold Medalist got married to fellow gymnast Bart Conner in
1996?

128
Who played Neo in the 1999 movie "The Matrix"?

129
What was the name of the TV Series, based on a movie of the same name, that
debuted in 1990 and starred Whoopi Goldberg and Jean Stapleton?

130
Who played the gay couple at the center of the movie "Philadelphia"?

131
In the movie "Indecent Proposal", how much money did John Cage offer to spend
the night with Diana Murphy?

125
"A Chorus Line"

126
"The City"

127
Nadia Comaneci

128
Keanu Reeves

129
"Bagdad Café"

130
Tom Hanks and Antonio Banderas

131
One Million Dollars

132
Who starred as the three Drag Queens in the 1995 movie "To Wong Foo, Thanks for Everything! Julie Newmar"?

133
Who got her start in Show Business as a Fly Girl on the sketch Comedy Show "In Living Color"?

134
What Prime Time Soap Opera was a spin-off of "Beverly Hills, 90210" and centered around the residents of an apartment complex in Los Angeles?

135
What 1995 movie directed by Ron Howard starred Tom Hanks, Kevin Bacon and Bill Paxton?

136
What 1990 Musical TV Series about a group of Los Angeles cops was canceled after only eleven episodes?

137
Who played the title role in the TV Series "Blossom"?

138
What Savage Garden song mentions "A Chic-A-Cherry Cola"?

132
Patrick Swayze, John Leguizamo and Wesley Snipes

133
Jennifer Lopez

134
"Melrose Place"

135
"Apollo 13"

136
"Cop Rock"

137
Mayim Bialik

138
"I Want You"

139

What Salt-N Pepa song says the line "I Don't Think They're Going to Play This on The Radio"?

140

Which "Friends" cast member starred on the short-lived "Married...With Children" spin-off "Top of the Heap"?

141

What was the name of the actress that Julia Roberts played in the movie "Notting Hill"?

142

What song was played on "The Fresh Prince of Bel-Air" for the Carlton dance?

143

What movie features the line "You're Killing Me Smalls"?

144

Who had a number two hit in America with the song "Rico Suave"?

145

Who played Dr. Hannibal Lecter in the 1991 movie "The Silence of the Lambs"?

146
In 1992, who was Johnny Carson's last guest when he ended his run on "The Tonight Show"?

147
Which two actors played the characters that switch faces in the movie "Face/Off"?

148
What file sharing service started in 1999 that let users download music for free?

149
What TV Show that started in 1993 follows Cory Matthews and his family and friends?

150
What song does Adam Sandler sing into the intercom when his girlfriend leaves him in the movie "Happy Gilmore"?

151
What band released the 1998 album "Celebrity Skin"?

152
What was the name of the prison drama that started in 1997 on HBO and had Ernie Hudson playing the warden?

153
Who played Claudia Salinger on the TV Series "Party of Five"?

154
In the movie "Pretty Woman", what Opera makes Julia Robert's character cry?

155
Who won the World Series in 1990?

156
What was the name of the TV Series that debuted in 1996 starring John Lithgow and revolved around four aliens sent to Earth?

157
What was the last name of Lyle and Erik, the brothers who were convicted of killing their parents in 1996?

158
Who played the title role in the TV Series "Moesha"?

159
What was the name of the strip club in the HBO Series "The Sopranos"?

153
Lacey Chabert

154
"La Traviata"

155
Cincinnati Reds

156
"3rd Rock from The Sun"

157
Menendez

158
Brandy Norwood

159
Bada Bing

160

Who was the first female commanding officer on a "Star Trek" Series when "Star Trek: Voyager" debuted in 1995?

161

In what city does "Sex and the City" take place?

162

What computer product was launched with a commercial featuring The Rolling Stones song "Start Me Up"?

163

Who played the cable installer in the film "The Cable Guy"?

164

In 1994, what did cyclist Miguel Indurain win?

165

What was the name of the first Aaron Spelling daytime Soap Opera that debuted in 1996 and ran until 1999?

166

Who played Nina Banks in the film "Father of the Bride"?

160

Captain Kathryn Janeway played by Kate Mulgrew

161

New York City

162

Windows 95

163

Jim Carrey

164

The Tour de France

165

"Sunset Beach"

166

Diane Keaton

167
What was the name of the 1994 film that starred Winona Ryder, Ethan Hawk and Ben Stiller and marked Stiller's first turn as a film director?

168
What was the name of the stuffed animals that became an internet sensation when people started to buy and sell for high prices in the 90s?

169
What were the names of the three James Bond movies released in the 1990s?

170
Which baseball player got married to and then divorced actress Halle Berry?

171
What was the name of the 1996 album by Alanis Morissette that sold over 30 million copies worldwide?

172
What music video features a girl dressed like a bee dancing to a Blind Melon song?

173
What was the name of the 1990 film starring Jeff Daniels and John Goodman that centers around a California town with a spider problem?

167

"Reality Bites"

168

Beanie Babies

169

"Goldeneye", "Tomorrow Never Dies" and "The World Is Not Enough"

170

David Justice

171

"Jagged Little Pill"

172

"No Rain"

173

"Arachnophobia"

174

Who wrote the book and newspaper column that became the TV Series "Sex and The City"?

175

Who played Angela Chase on the TV show "My So-Called Life"?

176

Who became the head coach of the Miami Dolphins in 1996 after Don Shula retired?

177

What TV show produced the number one song "How Do You Talk to An Angel" in 1992?

178

Who directed the 1990 film "Edward Scissorhands"?

179

What was the name of the 1997 horror movie that starred Jennifer Love Hewitt, Sarah Michelle Gellar, Ryan Phillippe and Freddie Prinze Jr.?

180

What was the item that became the must have toy for the 1996 Christmas shopping season and caused consumers to get into fights when stores ran out of stock?

181

Who released the 1996 song "They Don't Care About Us"?

182

What Queen song did Liza Minnelli sing at the Freddie Mercury Tribute Concert
at Wembley Stadium in London?

183

In the movie "Mr. Wonderful", what kind of business did Matt Dillion's character
Gus want to buy?

184

What were the names of the three members of the group TLC?

185

What singer played Tiny, who worked at the heavy metal bar The Gasworks in
the film "Wayne's World"?

186

Who directed the 1998 film "Rush Hour"?

187

What was Rachel's middle name on "Friends"?

181

Michael Jackson

182

"We Are the Champions"

183

A bowling alley

184

Tionne "T–Boz" Watkins, Lisa "Left Eye" Lopez and Rozonda "Chili" Thomas

185

Meatloaf

186

Brett Ratner

187

Karen

188
What Royal couple divorced in 1996?

189
What two actors played Armand and Albert in the film "The Birdcage"?

190
The Musical group SWV hit number six on the American charts with the song "I'm So into You". What did the letters SWV stand for?

191
What was the name of the MC Hammer song released in 1990 that used a Rick James sample?

192
Where were the 1998 Commonwealth Games held?

193
Which member of "The Real World: San Francisco" died just hours after the season finale aired?

194
What song by Lou Bega mentions the names Monica, Erica, Rita, Tina, Sandra, Mary and Jessica?

188
Prince Charles and Princess Diana

189
Robin Williams and Nathan Lane

190
Sisters With Voices

191
"U Can't Touch This"

192
Kuala Lumpur, Malaysia

193
Pedro Zamora

194
"Mambo No. 5 (A Little Bit Of...)"

195
What 1994 music video by Madonna featured a bullfighter?

196
What was the name of the TV Comedy Series that featured Tim Daly and Steven Weber as brothers that own a small airline?

197
What Tom Hanks movie was made into a Broadway Musical that opened and closed in 1996?

198
What was the name of the Children's Television Series that launched in the late 90s and included the characters Tinky-Winky, Dipsy, Laa Laa and Po?

199
Who hosted the 67th Academy Awards in 1995 that was trashed by most critics after he made a joke about introducing Oprah Winfrey and Uma Thurman that fell flat?

200
Who won his first Golf Masters title in 1997?

201
What former MTV VJ starred in the 1994 movie "Blank Check"?

195
"Take A Bow"

196
"Wings"

197
"Big"

198
"Teletubbies"

199
David Letterman

200
Tiger Woods

201
Karen "Duff" Duffy

202
What animated TV show aired its 100ᵗʰ episode in 1994?

203
Who played Diana Murphy in the 1993 movie "Indecent Proposal"?

204
Who directed the 1997 film "Titanic"?

205
What actor and actress won the top acting Oscars for their roles in "As Good as It Gets"?

206
In 1992, what was the only Grand Slam Tennis tournament that Monica Seles did not win?

207
Which member of "Star Trek: The Next Generation" directed the 1998 film "Star Trek: Insurrection"?

208
What Sitcom aired the episode "The Contest" in 1992?

202
"The Simpsons"

203
Demi Moore

204
James Cameron

205
Jack Nicholson and Helen Hunt

206
Wimbledon

207
Jonathan Frakes

208
"Seinfeld"

209

What country artist released the song "Friends in Low Places" from his album "No Fences"?

210

In 1990, who played Tess McGill on the short-lived TV Series "Working Girl" based on the movie starring Melanie Griffith?

211

Who released her "MTV Unplugged" CD and concert which featured the number one song "I'll Be There", a Jackson 5 cover with Trey Lorenz?

212

Who starred opposite Michelle Pfeiffer in the 1996 movie "Up Close and Personal"?

213

In the 1991 song "Unbelievable" by EMF, which comedian was featured in a sampled sound bite?

214

In 1990, who sang the National Anthem at a San Diego Padres games that caused public outrage after the singer screeched through the song and then grabbed her crotch and spit?

209
Garth Brooks

210
Sandra Bullock

211
Mariah Carey

212
Robert Redford

213
Andrew "Dice" Clay

214
Roseanne Barr

215

Who directed the 1990 movie "Pretty Woman" starring Julia Roberts and Richard Gere?

216

In 1992, singer Rick Springfield starred in what short-lived TV Series?

217

In 1997, it was announced that scientists cloned the first sheep. What was the name of the animal?

218

What 90s song featured the lyrics "Really Wanna Zigazig Ah"?

219

What was the name of the Comedy Series that starred Molly Ringwald in 1996?

220

In 1998, which flamboyant singer was knighted by Queen Elizabeth?

221

Who played the title role in the TV Series "Nash Bridges"?

215
Garry Marshall

216
"Human Target"

217
Dolly

218
"Wannabe" by The Spice Girls

219
"Townies"

220
Elton John

221
Don Johnson

222

At the very beginning of the 1995 film "Jumanji", what year is flashed on the screen?

223

What film features the line "Life Is Like a Box of Chocolates"?

224

What was the name of the spin-off TV Show from "Melrose Place" that starred Linda Gray?

225

What band was singing about "Counting Blue Cars" in 1995?

226

What "Saturday Night Live" star was murdered by his wife in 1998, who then took her own life?

227

Who played Grace on the TV Series "Grace Under Fire"?

222
1869

223
"Forest Gump"

224
"Models Inc."

225
Dishwalla

226
Phil Hartman

227
Brett Butler

228

What was the name of the Dance TV Series that debuted on MTV in 1992 and was hosted by "The Real World" star Eric Nies?

229

What 1991 song from The Scorpions sings about Gorky Park?

230

Who first won the Tour de France in 1999, but was later stripped of the title for using performance-enhancing drugs?

231

Who played Shooter McGavin in the 1996 film "Happy Gilmore"?

232

What two Musical acts did the song "One Sweet Day", that spent 16 weeks at the top of the Billboard Hot 100 Chart?

233

What agreement between the United States, Canada and Mexico went into effect on January 1, 1994?

234

What singer released the album "Tuesday Night Music Club" in 1993?

235

Who played Gloria Clemente in the 1992 Movie "White Men Can't Jump?

236

Who played Kim Boggs in the film "Edward Scissorhands"?

237

What TV Series started in 1990 that ran for ten years and featured a famous
California zip code?

238

Which man won the Golf U.S. Open in 1999?

239

Who sang the theme song "Closer to Free" from the TV Series "Party of Five"?

240

What was the name of the park where a bomb exploded during the 1996 Summer
Olympics?

234
Sheryl Crow

235
Rosie Perez

236
Winona Ryder

237
"Beverly Hills, 90210"

238
Payne Stewart

239
BoDeans

240
Centennial Olympic Park

241
What song is featured in the opening scene of the movie "The Birdcage"?

242
Who was the first female Security of State when she took office in 1997?

243
What remix of a 1992 by TLC gave the group Outkast their first major record label
appearance?

244
What Madonna movie featured the song "This Used to Be My Playground"?

245
In the film "Four Weddings and a Funeral" who got married at the first wedding?

246
Where were the 1998 Winter Olympic games held?

247
What duo made up the Music Group Savage Garden?

248
Which member of The Spice Girls left the group in 1998, just before their first tour of the United States?

249
What was the name of the Swedish Pop group that did the song "The Sign"?

250
Who starred as Jack Ryan in the 1990 film "The Hunt for Red October"?

251
In 1996, which NBA team set a record when they won 72 games in a season?

252
What was the name of the number one song from Celine Dion that came from the movie "Up Close and Personal"?

253
Who played "Buffy the Vampire Slayer" on the TV Series that began in 1997?

254
What singer had a hit with her 1991 debut song "Finally", which was featured three years later in the movie "The Adventures of Priscilla: Queen of the Desert"?

248

Geri Halliwell (Ginger Spice)

249

Ace Of Base

250

Alec Baldwin

251

The Chicago Bulls

252

"Because You Loved Me"

253

Sarah Michelle Gellar

254

CeCe Peniston

255

What 1996 film starred Neve Campbell as Sidney Prescott?

256

What radio personality was the subject of the movie "Private Parts"?

257

What TV Comedy Show began in 1996 starring Ray Romano?

258

Who did Whitney Houston marry in 1992?

259

Who played the title role in the 1997 movie "Selena"?

260

What was the name of the TV Series that started in 1993 and starred Queen Latifah and Kim Fields?

261

What was the name of Meat Loaf's only number one song that topped the U.S. charts in 1993?

255
"Scream"

256
Howard Stern

257
"Everybody Loves Raymond"

258
Bobby Brown

259
Jennifer Lopez

260
"Living Single"

261
"I'd Do Anything for Love (But I Won't Do That)"

262

In 1995, who was the Speaker of The United States House of Representatives?

263

What was the name of the debut solo single from Jon Bon Jovi that hit number one in 1990 and was featured in the movie "Young Guns II"?

264

What was the name of the 1999 spin-off from "Party of Five" that starred Jennifer Love Hewitt and Jennifer Garner that only ran for one season?

265

What song made famous by Roberta Flack did The Fugees remake in 1996?

266

Who won the Best Actress Oscar in 1993 at the 65th Academy Awards for her role in the film "Howards End"?

267

What musical instrument brings Jack to life in the 1998 film "Jack Frost"?

268

Who played Chandler's mother on the TV Series "Friends"?

269
Who sang the song "Crush" that was released in 1998 and topped the charts in Canada, but only reached number three in the United States?

270
Which former Wimbledon Champion died in 1993 from AIDS?

271
What actress played Connie Doyle, who pretended to be Patricia Winterbourne in the movie "Mrs. Winterbourne"?

272
What was the original name of the first Harry Potter book released in 1997 in the United Kingdom?

273
Who played the older version of Rose in the movie "Titanic"?

274
What Queen song was featured in the movie "Wayne's World"?

275
What was the name of the lead singer of the band Pulp, who got into trouble at the 1996 Brit Awards when he went onstage during a performance by Michael Jackson?

269

Jennifer Paige

270

Arthur Ashe

271

Ricki Lake

272

"Harry Potter and The Philosopher's Stone"

273

Gloria Stuart

274

"Bohemian Rhapsody"

275

Jarvis Cocker

276

Who sang "I'll Be There for You", the theme song from the TV Series "Friends"?

277

What TV Series began in 1998 and starred Kevin James and Leah Remini as Doug and Carrie Heffernan?

278

What music video from The Spice Girls has Emma Bunton (Baby Spice), playing the part of Kung Fu Candy?

279

Who played the baseball scout in "A League of Their Own"?

280

Who did Hugh Grant's character Charles live with in the film "Four Weddings and a Funeral"?

281

How does Happy Gilmore's father die at the beginning of the movie?

282

What are the last names of Wayne and Garth in the movie "Wayne's World"?

276
The Rembrandts

277
"The King of Queens"

278
"Say You'll Be There"

279
Jon Lovitz

280
Scarlet

281
He gets hit by a hockey puck

282
Campbell and Algar

283

In 1993, Polly Klaas was kidnapped and later murdered in a California city that Winona Ryder grew up in. What was the city?

284

What was Tommy's last name on the animated Series "Rugrats"?

285

What two actors played the roles of Carter and Lee in the 1998 film "Rush Hour"?

286

Who directed the 1992 film "A League of Their Own"?

287

What Bruce Springsteen song won an Oscar for Best Original Song from a Tom Hanks movie?

288

What was the only "Rocky" movie released in the 1990s?

289

What sports star retired in 1991 after announcing that he was HIV Positive?

283
Petaluma

284
Pickles

285
Chris Tucker and Jackie Chan

286
Penny Marshall

287
"Streets of Philadelphia"

288
"Rocky V"

289
Magic Johnson

290

What movie features the line "Molly, you in danger girl"?

291

In the Sheryl Crow song "All I Wanna Do", what city does she mention in the spoken intro?

292

Who hosted the 49th Primetime Emmy Awards in 1997?

293

What song won Record of the Year at the Grammy Awards in 1992?

294

What recording effect did Cher use on vocals on her number one song "Believe" in 1998?

295

What band is usually featured on the t-shirt that Beavis wears on "Beavis and Butt-Head"?

296

In 1992, what country won The Cricket World Cup?

290
"Ghost"

291
L.A.

292
Bryant Gumbel

293
"Tears in Heaven" by Eric Clapton

294
Auto-Tune

295
Metallica

296
Pakistan

297
As the 1990s were ending, what was the term everyone was referring to as they feared all computers would shut down at the turn of the century?

298
Who won a Best Supporting Actress Oscar for her role in the film "My Cousin Vinny"?

299
What two siblings released the song "Scream" in 1995?

300
What Broadway show won the Tony for Best Musical in 1996?

301
Who played Cory Matthews on the TV Series "Boy Meets World"?

302
What was the highest grossing film of the 1990s?

303
What was the name of the only "Star Wars" movie released in the 90s?

304
What was the name of the 1993 film that has a boy trying to save an Orca Whale?

305
Who played the President in the movie "Independence Day"?

306
In the 1996 film "The Rock", what island does the title refer to?

307
Who was shot multiple times after attending a Mike Tyson boxing match in Las Vegas and died six days later?

308
Who played Susan Keane on the TV Series "Suddenly Susan"?

309
What song by The Righteous Brothers, originally released in 1965, gained new popularity after it appears in the 1990 film "Ghost"?

310
Where did a bomb go off in New York City on February 26, 1993, that killed six people?

304
"Free Willy"

305
Bill Pullman

306
Alcatraz

307
Tupac Shakur

308
Brooke Shields

309
"Unchained Melody"

310
The World Trade Center

311
What did the Clinton administration achieve in 1998 that hadn't happened in 30
years.

312
What song did Puff Daddy release as a tribute to The Notorious B.I.G. that
featured a sample of The Police's "Every Breath You Take"?

313
What California area code was created in November of 1991 that split up the 213
area code?

314
What was the name of the album released by George Michael in 1990 that
featured the number one song "Praying for Time"?

315
Where were the 1994 Winter Olympics held?

316
What song by Seal was featured in the movies "The Never-Ending Story III" and
"Batman Forever"?

317
Who played Justice in the 1993 movie "Poetic Justice"?

311
A budget surplus

312
"I'll Be Missing You"

313
Area code 310

314
"Listen Without Prejudice Vol. 1"

315
Lillehammer, Norway

316
"Kiss From a Rose"

317
Janet Jackson

318

Who released the album "Yes I Am", which featured the song "Come to My Window" in 1993?

319

What was the name of the 1991 film directed by Martin Scorsese that starred Robert De Niro and Nick Nolte?

320

Which boxer came out of retirement in 1994 and became the oldest World Heavyweight Champion in history?

321

Who played the three witches in the 1993 movie "Hocus Pocus"?

322

Who played the title role of "Ally McBeal" that debuted in 1997?

323

In 1999, who was elected the Prime Minister of New Zealand?

324

What 1991 music video from Paula Abdul featured Keanu Reeves in a "Rebel Without a Cause" storyline?

318
Melissa Etheridge

319
"Cape Fear"

320
George Foreman

321
Bette Midler, Sarah Jessica Parker and Kathy Najimy

322
Calista Flockhart

323
Helen Clark

324
"Rush Rush"

325
What were the first names of the six "Friends" from the TV Series?

326
What was the name of the pre-historic TV Series centered around the Sinclair family and featured the voices of Stuart Pankin, Sherman Hemsley and Sally Struthers?

327
Who played the title character on "The Larry Sanders Show"?

328
In 1993, which country lost their National Soccer team in a plane crash while traveling to the World Cup Qualifiers?

329
What was the name of the 1992 film that starred Stephen Rea, Jaye Davison and Forest Whitaker and features a theme song by Boy George?

330
Which eleven-year-old won the Best Supporting Actress Oscar at the Academy Awards in 1994 for her role in the film "The Piano"?

325
Monica, Phoebe, Rachel, Chandler, Joey and Ross

326
"Dinosaurs"

327
Garry Shandling

328
Zambia

329
"The Crying Game"

330
Anna Paquin

331
What music event took place about 100 miles north of New York City in 1994 that featured Aerosmith, Metallica, Nine Inch Nail, Sheryl Crow and Joe Cocker?

332
What category was the tornado that struck at the end of the movie "Twister"?

333
What happened to Bill Clinton on December 19, 1998?

334
What remake of an Eric Carmen song did Celine Dion release in 1996?

335
Who played the Taylors, the couple at the center of the TV Series "Home Improvement"?

336
Which professional golfer died in a plane crash in 1999?

337
Who won the Best Performance by a Leading Actor in a Musical at the 45th Tony Awards in 1991?

331
Woodstock '94

332
F5

333
He was impeached

334
"All By Myself"

335
Tim Allen and Patricia Richardson

336
Payne Stewart

337
Jonathan Pryce for "Miss Saigon"

338
What 1991 movie starring Robin Williams has a scene that features hundreds of couples waltzing in Grand Central Station in New York City?

339
What award show debuted in 1995 and honors actors in television and film?

340
Who directed the film "The Prince of Tides"?

341
Who played the T-1000 in the movie "Terminator 2: Judgement Day"?

342
Who won her one and only singles Gram Slam tennis title by defeating Martina Navratilova at Wimbledon in 1994?

343
What band released the album "(What's the Story) Morning Glory" that featured the song "Wonderwall"?

344
What singer caused public outrage after appearing on "Saturday Night Live" in 1992, when she tore up a picture of Pope John Paul II?

345
What spin-off from "Beavis and Butthead" made its debut in March of 1997 on MTV?

346
Who starred as Batman in the 1995 movie "Batman Forever"?

347
In 1999, what closed above 11,000 for the first time?

348
What group released the song "Whoomp! (There it is)" in 1993?

349
Who directed the 1998 movie "Saving Private Ryan" starring Tom Hanks and Matt Damon?

350
What audio format came out in 1991 and started the file sharing frenzy?

351
Which two players won the final Grand Slam Tennis championship of the 1990s in singles?

345
"Daria"

346
Val Kilmer

347
The Dow Jones

348
Tag Team

349
Steven Spielberg

350
MP3

351
Andre Agassi and Serena Williams at the U.S. Open

352
What singer was featured on the TV Series "Ally McBeal" as herself?

353
What Formula One driver was killed in an accident at the 1994 San Marino Grand Prix?

354
In what state did the TV Series "Evening Shade" take place?

355
What was the name of the Variety TV Series that starred Britney Spears, Justin Timberlake, Christina Aguilera and Ryan Gosling in the 90s?

356
What were the names of the five Backstreet Boys?

357
Who played the title character in 1993 film "What's Eating Gilbert Grape"?

352
Vonda Shepard

353
Ayrton Senna

354
Arkansas

355
"The All-New Mickey Mouse Club"

356
A.J. McLean, Howie Dorough, Nick Carter, Kevin Richardson and Brian Littrell

357
Johnny Depp

358

What singer released the 1992 song "Hazard", which told the story of a woman named Mary who disappeared?

359

In the movie "Speed", what speed can the bus not fall below, or it would explode?

360

What team did Fernando Valenzuela play for in 1990 when he threw a no-hitter?

361

What singer released a cover version of Bonnie Tyler's "Total Eclipse of the Heart" in 1995 that reached number two in the United States?

362

What was the name of the coffee house on "Friends"?

363

What animated Disney movie was released in 1991 and featured the voices of Robby Benson, Jerry Orbach and Angela Lansbury?

358
Richard Marx

359
Fifty Miles Per Hour

360
The Los Angeles Dodgers

361
Nicki French

362
Central Perk

363
"Beauty and the Beast"

364
Who did Julia Roberts marry in 1993, only to divorce him a few years later?

365
What TV Series had cops investigating a crime and the district attorney trying the case, that debuted in 1990 and would run for decades?

366
In 1995, which country won the FIFA Women's World Cup that was held in Sweden?

367
Who won the Tony Award in 1993 for her role in the Musical "Kiss of the Spider Woman"?

368
Which Spice Girl released her debut solo record, "Northern Star" in the last months of the 90s?

369
In 1991 the documentary film "Madonna: Truth or Dare" was released in America, however it had a different title outside the USA. What was it called?

370
What band consisting of three brothers known for Disco music was inducted into the Rock and Roll Hall of Fame in 1997?

364
Lyle Lovett

365
"Law and Order"

366
Norway

367
Chita Rivera

368
Melanie C (Sporty Spice)

369
"In Bed with Madonna"

370
The Bee Gees

371

What 1991 film starred Sally Field as aging Soap Opera star Celeste Talbert?

372

Who was the Governor of California from 1991 to 1999?

373

Who played the title roles in the movie "Thelma and Louise?

374

Who released the song "Millennium" that went number one in the UK, but only managed to hit number 72 in the United States?

375

What 1997 movie featured an on-screen kiss between Kevin Kline and Tom Selleck?

376

In 1994, what Hockey team won the Stanley Cup at Madison Square Garden?

377

Who was assassinated in Tel Aviv on November 4, 1995?

371

"Soap Dish"

372

Pete Wilson

373

Geena Davis and Susan Sarandon

374

Robbie Williams

375

"In & Out"

376

The New York Rangers

377

Yitzhak Rabin

378

In what Musical did Petula Clark make her Broadway debut, starring alongside
Shaun and David Cassidy?

379

What Swedish duo had a number one hit in America with the 1991 song
"Joyride"?

380

Who played Tina Turner in the 1993 film "What's Love Got to Do with It"?

381

Which NBA star was a first-round draft pick in 1992 and joined the Orlando
Magic?

382

What David E. Kelley legal drama debuted in 1997 and starred Dylan McDermott
as Bobby Donnell?

383

Who were the five members of the Boy Band *NSYNC?

384

What movie did Tom Cruise make in 1993 that was based on a John Grisham
book?

378
"Blood Brothers"

379
Roxette

380
Angela Bassett

381
Shaquille O'Neal

382
"The Practice"

383
Lance Bass, JC Chasez, Joey Fatone, Chris Kirkpatrick and Justin Timberlake

384
"The Firm"

385
In 1997, what song did Aqua release that led to a lawsuit from Mattel?

386
What currency was introduced in the 1990s and is used by France, Ireland, Italy and about twenty others?

387
In what city did a bomb explode at the Alfred Murrah Federal Building on April 19, 1995?

388
What was the name of the 1992 film that starred Meryl Streep, Bruce Willis and Goldie Hawn?

389
Who played "The Nanny" on the CBS Sitcom?

390
Who joined Manchester United in 1992 when he was 17 years old?

391
What Washington, DC Mayor was arrested in 1990 for crack cocaine possession?

392
What one-hit wonder band released the track "What's Up" in 1992?

393
Who played "Dick Tracy" in the 1990 movie?

394
What was the name of the song by Haddaway that was released in 1993 and was featured in the 1998 movie "A Night at the Roxbury"?

395
What actor collapsed on the sidewalk outside the L.A. Club The Viper Room and later died at Cedars-Sinai Medical Center?

396
What band released the 1996 album "Tragic Kingdom" that featured the single "Don't Speak"?

397
What Musical opened on Broadway in 1997, based on a 1994 film and featured music by Elton John?

392
4 Non Blondes

393
Warren Beatty

394
"What Is Love"

395
River Phoenix

396
No Doubt

397
"The Lion King"

398
Who played bodyguard Frank Farmer in the movie "The Bodyguard"?

399
Which former President died in 1994, about ten months after his wife passed away?

400
What Girl Group released their first single in 1997 with the song "No, No, No"?

401
What 1995 movie stars Sandra Bullock as a transit worker in Chicago?

402
What song by Santana was released in September 1999 and sings about Spanish Harlem?

403
What Science Fiction TV show launched in 1997 and starred Richard Dean Anderson?

404
What band released the 1995 record "These Days" which was the first to feature new bassist Hugh McDonald, who replaced original member Alec John Such?

398
Kevin Costner

399
Richard Nixon

400
Destiny's Child

401
"While You Were Sleeping"

402
"Maria Maria"

403
"Stargate SG-1"

404
Bon Jovi

405
In 1998, what band sang about being "Pretty Fly (For a White Guy)"?

406
What two baseball teams were added when the National League expanded in 1993?

407
What company was launched in 1994 by Jeff Bezos?

408
What was the name of the character that Tom Hanks voiced in "Toy Story"?

409
What were the names of the three Banks children on "The Fresh Prince of Bel-Air"?

410
What Paula Cole song asks the question "Where is my Marlboro Man"?

411
What drug was introduced in the late 90s to help men with erectile dysfunction?

412
What were the character names that David Duchovny and Gillian Anderson
played on "The X-Files"?

413
What 1994 song by Lisa Loeb was featured in the movie "Reality Bites"?

414
What Musical made its Broadway debut in 1991 and featured a scene with a
helicopter landing on stage?

415
What band released the record "Cracked Rear View" that featured the song "Hold
My Hand"?

416
What was the name of the TV Series that began in 1998 that starred James Van
Der Beek, Katie Holmes and Michelle Williams?

417
What was launched into space in 1990 and still operational decades later?

412
Fox Mulder and Dana Scully

413
"Stay (I Missed You)"

414
"Miss Saigon"

415
Hootie & the Blowfish

416
"Dawson's Creek"

417
The Hubble Space Telescope

418
Who won an Oscar for playing Marge Gunderson in the movie "Fargo"?

419
What band featuring former Bananarama singer Siobhan Fahey released the song "Stay" in 1992?

420
In what city does the TV Series "Frasier" take place?

421
What was the name of the 1999 movie starring Sarah Michelle Gellar, Ryan Phillippe, Selma Blair and Reese Witherspoon?

422
Who sang the 1996 song "Barely Breathing"?

423
In 1993, who became the first female Prime Minster of Canada?

424
What is the stage name of Norman Cook, who had a hit with his song "Praise You"?

418
Frances McDormand

419
Shakespears Sister

420
Seattle

421
"Cruel Intentions"

422
Duncan Sheik

423
Kim Campbell

424
Fatboy Slim

425
What were the first names of the three brothers from Hanson, who had a number one song with "MMMBop" in 1997?

426
Who played the married couple in the 1994 movie "True Lies"?

427
What Weezer song was also the name of a 1950's singer that died in a plane crash?

428
What was the name of the woman, played by Martin Lawrence, who lived across the hall from him on the TV Series "Martin"?

429
Who played the gay best friend George in the 1997 movie "My Best Friend's Wedding"?

430
Who released the 1999 song "Genie in a Bottle"?

431
What was the first book selected for Oprah's Book Club in September 1996?

425
Isaac, Taylor and Zac

426
Arnold Schwarzenegger and Jamie Lee Curtis

427
"Buddy Holly"

428
Sheneneh

429
Rupert Everett

430
Christina Aguilera

431
"The Deep End of the Ocean" by Jacquelyn Mitchard

432
Who played President Tom Beck in the movie "Deep Impact"?

433
What Broadway Musical did Bebe Neuwirth win a Tony Award for her role as
Velma Kelly?

434
What was the name of Dr. Dre's first solo record, released in 1992, after he left
N.W.A.?

435
In what state was Columbine High School, where a school shooting took place on
April 20, 1999?

436
What 1991 album cover features a naked baby boy swimming underwater and a
dollar bill on a fishhook?

437
What was the full title of the third "Die Hard" movie that was released in 1995?

438
What Musical Act released the 1996 song "C'Mon N' Ride It (The Train)"?

432
Morgan Freeman

433
"Chicago"

434
"The Chronic"

435
Colorado

436
"Nevermind" by Nirvana

437
"Die Hard with a Vengeance"

438
Quad City DJ'S

439
What Chaka Khan song did Whitney Houston remake for "The Bodyguard" soundtrack?

440
Who played the angel Seth in the 1998 movie "City of Angels"?

441
Who won the Tony award in 1999 for his role as Willy Loman in "Death of a Salesman"?

442
Who became the first black woman to win the Nobel Prize in Literature in 1993?

443
All-4-One released the songs "I Swear" and "I Can Love You Like That" that were both originally done by which County Music artist?

444
Who performed "La Copa De La Vida (The Cup of Life) at the 1999 Grammy Awards that impressed Madonna so much that she jumped on stage in the press room to meet him?

445
Which Musical Artist broke her back in a tour bus accident in Pennsylvania in 1990?

439
"I'm Every Woman"

440
Nicholas Cage

441
Brian Dennehy

442
Toni Morrison

443
John Michael Montgomery

444
Ricky Martin

445
Gloria Estefan

446
Who starred as Darby Shaw in the 1993 movie "The Pelican Brief"?

447
What TV Series starring Kyle MacLachlan follows the investigation into the murder of Laura Palmer?

448
What 1997 song tells you "Oh My God, We're Back Again"?

449
What TV Series ended on May 14, 1998, and saw the four main characters going to jail?

450
Who played the character of John Munch that first appeared on the TV Series "Homicide: Life on the Street" and then moved over to "Law and Order: Special Victims Unit"?

451
What storm killed over 11,000 people in Honduras and Nicaragua in 1998?

452
Which hair metal band released the song "Something to Believe in" that hit number four in America in 1990?

446
Julia Roberts

447
"Twin Peaks"

448
"Everybody (Backstreet's Back)" by Backstreet Boys

449
"Seinfeld"

450
Richard Belzer

451
Hurricane Mitch

452
Poison

453
What movie and television review website launched in 1998?

454
What song by The Bloodhound Gang mentions The Discovery Channel?

455
Which member of The Eurythmics released the 1992 album "Diva" that featured the songs "Walking on Broken Glass" and "Why"?

456
What was the name of the hotel and casino in the 1995 movie "Casino"?

457
Who ran for President of the United States in both 1992 and 1996 outside of the two-party system and failed to win a single state in either election?

458
What was the name of the song that Mariah Carey and Whitney Houston released in 1998?

459
What was the name of the 1992 movie starring Bridget Fonda and Jennifer Jason Leigh?

453
Rotten Tomatoes

454
"The Bad Touch"

455
Annie Lennox

456
The Tangiers Casino

457
Ross Perot

458
"When You Believe"

459
"Single White Female"

460
Which film director died in 1998 while driving on the Long Island Expressway in New York, when a metal pipe crashed through his windshield and struck him in the head?

461
What Culture Club song does George sing in the movie "The Wedding Singer"?

462
Who directed the movie "Malcolm X" that starred Denzel Washington?

463
Which baseball team won the 1993 World Series?

464
What band released the song "All Star" in 1999?

465
What 1997 song by Shania Twain mentions Brad Pitt?

466
Which actor made his film debut in the movie "Clueless" playing Josh Lucas?

460
Alan J. Pakula

461
"Do You Really Want to Hurt Me?"

462
Spike Lee

463
Toronto Blue Jays

464
Smash Mouth

465
"That Don't Impress Me Much"

466
Paul Rudd

467

What phone company hired Whitney Houston to sing its promotional campaign titled "Your True Voice" in the mid-90s?

468

What 1995 film stars Leonardo DiCaprio as Jim Carroll, a high school student addicted to drugs?

469

What beer was introduced in 1993 and featured commercials that warned you to beware of the penguins?

470

Who finally won a Daytime Emmy Award in 1999 after being nominated 19 times?

471

Who was the judge that presided over the O.J. Simpson criminal trial in 1995?

472

Who played Captain Frank Ramsey in the film "Crimson Tide"?

473

What was the name of the instrumental song by Robert Miles that went number one in over a dozen countries, but only hit number 21 in America?

467
AT&T

468
"The Basketball Diaries"

469
Bud Ice

470
Susan Lucci

471
Judge Lance Ito

472
Gene Hackman

473
"Children"

474
Who was the comedian who starred in commercials for The Polaroid One Step
Talking Camera that was introduced in 1995?

475
What clear, carbonated alcoholic beverage did the Coors Brewing Company unveil
in 1993?

476
What two teams were created during the 1998 Major League Baseball expansion?

477
What three actresses played the main members of "The First Wives Club"?

478
What singer from The B-52s was featured on the 1991 song "Shiny Happy
People" from R.E.M.?

479
What actress returned for the finale in her role as Barbara Weston on the TV
Series "Empty Nest" in 1995?

480
What actor was shot and killed in 1993 during the filming of the movie "The
Crow"?

474
Sinbad

475
Zima

476
Tampa Bay Devil Rays and Arizona Diamondbacks

477
Bette Midler, Goldie Hawn and Diane Keaton

478
Kate Pierson

479
Kristy McNichol

480
Brandon Lee

481
In 1993, who became the first woman to serve as the Attorney General of the
United States?

482
Who was at the controls of a small plane when it crashed in 1999, killing the
pilot, his wife and sister-in-law?

483
What was the name of the song by Los del Rio that spent 14 weeks at the top of
the American charts and started a new dance craze?

484
In 1997, which boxer did Mike Tyson bite, tearing off part of his ear?

485
What were the four first names of the women at the center of the TV Series "Sex
and the City" that made its debut on HBO in 1998?

486
What was the name of the Britney Spears debut song and album that launched
her career in 1999?

487
What was the Airline and flight number of the plane that crashed into the
Atlantic Ocean near Long Island, shortly after takeoff from JFK enroute to Paris in
1996?

481
Janet Reno

482
John F. Kennedy Jr.

483
"Macarena"

484
Evander Holyfield

485
Carrie, Charlotte, Miranda and Samantha

486
"...Baby One More Time"

487
TWA 800

488

What was the name of the six-year-old girl that was murdered at her home in Colorado in 1996 that dominated headlines for years?

489

What TV comedy Series concluded in 1993 and saw the return of Shelley Long in her role as Diane Chambers?

490

In 1999, Will Smith had both a Number One song and Movie that shared a name. What was it?

491

Which mobster dubbed "The Teflon Don" was convicted in 1992 of murder and racketeering charges?

492

What video game console was released in 1991 in America and came with the game Super Mario World?

493

Which religious figure passed away in 1997 in Calcutta?

488
JonBenet Ramsey

489
"Cheers"

490
"Wild Wild West"

491
John Gotti

492
Super Nintendo

493
Mother Teresa

494
In the 1990 movie "Home Alone", where were the McCallister family traveling to when Kevin was left behind?

495
Which Scottish woman is the lead singer of the band Garbage?

496
Which Space Shuttle was destroyed during a meteor shower at the beginning of the movie "Armageddon"?

497
What 1990 book by Michael Crichton became a movie directed by Steven Spielberg in 1993?

498
What band released the 1997 album "OK Computer"?

499
What was the last name of Paul and Jamie on the TV Series "Mad About You"?

500
What was the last number one song of the 1990s on the Billboard Hot 100 Chart?

494
Paris

495
Shirley Manson

496
Atlantis

497
"Jurassic Park"

498
Radiohead

499
Buchman

500
"Smooth" by Santana. Featuring Rob Thomas